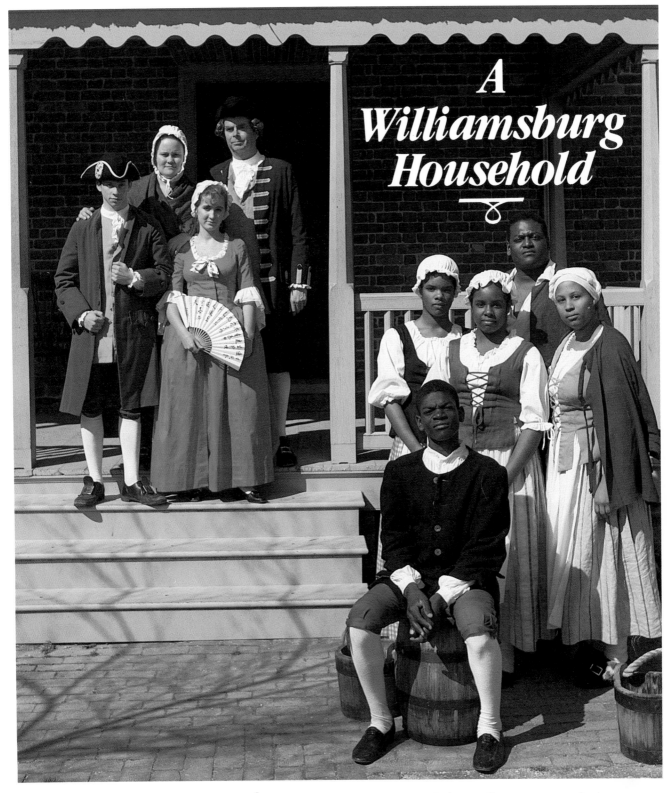

A Williamsburg Household

by Joan Anderson | Photographed by George Ancona

Clarion Books/Ticknor & Fields: A Houghton Mifflin Company/New York

Anderson

Clarion Books
Ticknor & Fields, a Houghton Mifflin Company
Text copyright © 1988 by Joan Anderson
Photographs copyright © 1988 by George Ancona

Library of Congress Cataloging-in-Publication Data
Anderson, Joan
   A Williamsburg household / by Joan Anderson; photographed by
George Ancona.
         p.   cm.
   Summary: Focuses on events in the household of a white family and
its black slaves in Colonial Williamsburg in the eighteenth century.
   ISBN 0-89919-516-4
   [1. Slavery—Fiction.   2. Williamsburg (Va.)—Social life and
customs—Fiction.]   I. Ancona, George, ill.   II. Title.
PZ7.A5367Wi   1988
[Fic]—dc19   87-33803

In the servant quarters behind Wetherburn's Tavern, Rippon shivered in the cool morning air. It seemed he had only just gone to sleep, but already it was morning and time for Friday chores. He jumped up from his sleeping place near the hearth and stowed his straw-filled pallet in a corner. Quickly he buckled his shoes, threw on his jacket, and hurried across the courtyard into the tavern.

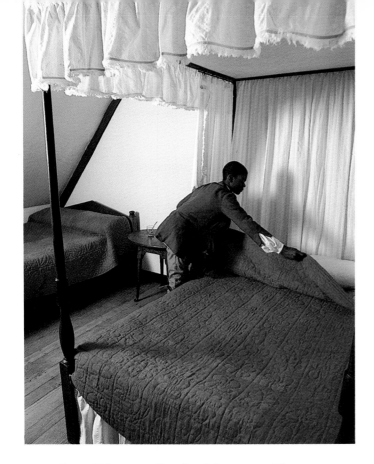

First, Rippon fetched logs and began to stoke the fires. Then he swabbed the bar before rushing into the Bull's Head Room to clean up after last night's party.

Although he got up each day before dawn and worked well into the night, Rippon couldn't possibly finish all the jobs that awaited him. Even so, he knew that if he rushed through his chores, he might get to attend the slave gathering tomorrow night in the Moody backyard.

Mr. Moody had sold Rippon off to Mr. Wetherburn a year ago. Before that, Rippon had lived at the Moody's with his two sisters and his mother, Cate. He was relieved that he had been spared the life of a field hand like his father, Samuel. Working in a tavern was easier than the backbreaking work in the field. Besides, Rippon loved eavesdropping on the patrons' conversations about events here in Virginia's capital. He was learning a great deal about the world and beginning to see how he could make his way in it, if he were clever.

Rippon finished straightening the guest rooms and was emptying chamber pots in the backyard when he heard an angry voice in the alleyway:

"Move along there, boy," the voice ordered. "I've better things to do than lead you off to your master for a lashing."

Rippon edged closer to the footway to see who the victim was this time.

"Aberdeen!" he exclaimed, recognizing one of Mr. Moody's slaves. "What'd you do?"

Aberdeen turned to answer, but the governor's servant pushed him on up the alley.

Rippon feared for Aberdeen ever since his friend had been hired out to work for the governor's footman. Everyone knew that once Aberdeen was on his own he would never be able to contain his simmering anger at slave life. This was Aberdeen's second offense. One more and he'd become a field hand for sure.

"I must tell Rose about her son," Rippon thought, his mind racing. But how? Slaves couldn't just wander away from their chores whenever they wanted to. Just then he noticed the vegetable carts making their way into town. It's market day, Rippon remembered. He would work in front of the tavern to catch his mother and Rose marketing.

Across town in the slave quarters behind the Moody house, Mistress Moody had just arrived to escort Rippon's mother off to market.

"Now then, Cate, I've brought you some rations," Mrs. Moody announced in a businesslike way. She placed a large bowl of beans and a pork shank on the table.

"Ain't often we get meat, Missus Moody," Cate said. "Is this some special occasion?"

"We needn't always wait for holiday time," the mistress answered, quite pleased with herself. "I know you like to flavor up the hominy."

"Mighty fine of you, ma'm," Cate said, a tinge of sarcasm in her voice.

"You'll see I've left some dresses in the laundry, things Hannah and I can't use anymore. Mister Moody insists that everyone in the household be dressed properly. I expect to see you wearing them soon. Now, one more thing. Here is a remedy for Molly." Mistress Moody held out a cup containing syrup of ginger. "I've heard her dreadful cough."

"Never you mind 'bout that, Missus," Cate countered. "We is using our own remedies."

"I know you are," Mrs. Moody continued, "but just to make sure, you give her one spoonful each day. You'll see, she'll soon throw it off."

"But Missus..." Cate interrupted.

"'Tis an order, Cate. We can't have you stepping away from the cooking to tend to Molly. Now then, let's be off to town."

Cate grabbed her shawl and a big basket and called to Rose to join them.

Rippon was sweeping the sidewalk in front of the tavern when he spotted the three women. His mother approached one of the farmers, insisting that his apples were bruised and the eggs weren't fresh. The more critical she became, the faster the price dropped. "Take any chance to impress the missus," Momma would tell Rippon and his sisters, Molly and Mary. "That way she give you more favors," Rippon recalled, as he saw the delight in Mrs. Moody's face.

In no time Rose and Cate had purchased two baskets
of produce, and Mrs. Moody had disappeared into the
bustling street. Rose and Cate hurried over to Rippon.

"You got no smile for yo' momma?" Cate asked when
she saw her son's serious expression. "What is yo'
problem, child? You ain't got yo'self in no trouble?"

"No, Momma, not me," Rippon replied quickly, "But
Aberdeen has."

"Aberdeen!" Rose gasped. "How do you know?"

"A footman brought him through here."

Rose clutched Cate's arm. "We must get back," she
said. "I've got to talk to him before Master Moody does.
That boy is powerful good at sassin' back when he is
mad. He might be in for more than a lashin' this time."

"All right, then," Cate said comfortingly. "We'll get
back to the house real quick."

Once back at the Moody house, Rose headed straight for the stable. It was the only building where Aberdeen could be detained. She looked through the window and found him sitting on a bale of hay.

"What has you done now, boy?" she asked.

"I ain't done nothin', Momma, really," he answered. "The footman blamed me for messin' up the horse's halter. I said I didn't do it. When he called me a liar, I called him one in return."

"You what?" Rose gasped.

"I had to, Momma. But when I did, he said I was talkin' back."

"Don't you know by now to keep yo' ears and eyes open and yo' mouth shut?" she asked.

"Everything will be all right, Momma, you'll see," Aberdeen said, trying to console her.

"One more lashin' and you'll land in the fields! Master Moody say so the last time. Ain't that enough to make you behave?"

"Don't you worry, Momma. I'm good at the work they give me. Besides, Mister Moody won't hit me hard. He knows I gots to work."

Just then Mrs. Moody called out in a shrill voice, "Rose! Rose! Are you out there?"

Rose began to run toward the courtyard.

"Why you let her talk to you that way, Momma?" Aberdeen called. "I'd tell her to hush her mouth." Rose stopped and turned toward her son.

"When you gon' face up to being a slave boy, Aberdeen?" his mother answered. "How many times I got to tell you that if we please the missus, all our needs is taken care of. You learn that, boy, or you will never last around here."

Rose turned away and ran to her angry mistress.

"Rose, where *have* you been?" Mrs. Moody was
scowling.

"I's…sorry, ma'm, I…," Rose began.

"Well, never mind explaining now," Mrs. Moody said
impatiently. "I do hope you mended Hannah's shawl
and laundered Daniel's shirt. The dancing teacher will
be here any minute."

"Yes, ma'm. I'll be just a minute, ma'm," Rose
mumbled as she ran to the laundry. Why hadn't she done
these things earlier this morning, she thought. She quickly
placed the iron by the hearth to heat it up and grabbed a
needle out of the sewing basket. Rush. Rush. Rush.
That's all she seemed to do. Being born a slave, she
thought, meant no relief.

After delivering the clothing to the main house, Rose dawdled a bit so that she could watch the lesson. The English dancing looked so strange to her. Both Daniel and Hannah were concentrating so hard on the intricate steps that it appeared they weren't having any fun at all. "At our gatherin's," Rose thought, "we just listen to the music and let our feet take us where they will."

On her way to the back door, she noticed Master Moody at his desk studying his account book. Mr. Moody, a tall, proud man, looked worried and drawn. She thought of approaching him to discuss Aberdeen's punishment. Then she heard him mumble something about his mounting debts and decided it was best to leave the matter for now. She quickly headed back to the laundry.

Piles of dirty shirts and breeches awaited her. As Rose added the clothes and boiling water to the wash kettle, she was haunted by Mr. Moody's mumblings. When the master got worried about money, he started selling things. Rose knew he wouldn't rid himself of his imported furniture for the house here in Williamsburg. And he would keep the newly purchased livestock and farm tools for his plantation several miles out of town. That left only the slaves to hire out or sell.

Rose envisioned Mr. Moody going over the list of domestic staff. Aberdeen would surely top the troublemaker list! Her heart pounded as she squeezed the water out of each garment, a process that made her feel momentarily powerful. Just then, her dark thoughts were broken as Cate began hollering at Mary and Molly.

"Molly! Get in here, girl. I 'spect to come home from market and find my kitchen all clean. You haven't done one thing."

"Here I is," Molly answered, coughing.

"Where has you been? The fire's almost out. Why, I had to fetch my own wood this mornin' and that is yo' job, child! Don't you know yo' poppa is comin' tomorrow night? If we get any more behind, there ain't no way we is gon' have time for him."

"I know, Momma."

"If you knows so much, then why don't you do like I say? Yo' poppa walks a good five miles after a long week in the field just so's he can visit," Cate continued.

"Don't worry so, Momma. We is gon' to be ready for Poppa."

"Where's yo' sister?"

"In the garden, Momma, gettin' the greens."

"Well at least I got me one good worker. You get out there too, y'hear."

Molly grabbed a basket and joined her sister.

"Bend your back, child," her mother shouted. "Who do you think you is? Some dainty lady that don't get herself dirty?"

Eventually the morning chores were finished. Now Cate and her daughters could get to the business of preparing rum cakes and apple tarts and all the other dishes needed for the weekend. As they worked, Mary gently broached the subject of school.

"Momma," she started out softly, "with all the work still to be done, do you think Missus Moody would let us stay out of school today?"

"Yeah," Molly jumped in, despising the hours spent memorizing the catechism with all those big words.

"You know Mistress Moody promised to send you to school every day of the week, and besides, I want you to learn to read so as you can teach us how good the Lord is," Cate replied.

"If he's so good, why do you suppose Poppa has to work so hard, Momma?" Molly asked, a feisty tone in her voice.

"Well, we ain't free, child, but we is alive, ain't we? And the master, he give us all that we need."

"Maybe he does and maybe he doesn't, Momma," Molly continued. "I betcha Aberdeen don't think he does. We was talkin' to him earlier and he sho' is angry."

"Never you mind 'bout that, you just leave him be. Now hurry up and finish those vegetables so you won't be late for school."

Soon after Molly and Mary left for school, Mr. Moody fetched Aberdeen. Rose was hanging up the laundry as they approached, but neither Aberdeen nor the master looked at her. They just walked by, heading straight for the backyard. The master was carrying a leather strap.

"Cate," Rose whispered, running to the kitchen door. "What shall we do? He's about to get his lashin'."

"There ain't nothin' you can do, child," Cate answered, putting her arm around her friend. "Just stay right here with me."

The two women could almost see the big oak tree where all the lashings were done. Cate held tight to Rose, who buried her head in her friend's bosom. The sounds of leather cracking against flesh and Aberdeen's cries filled the air.

In a few minutes all was quiet. Rose crept around the building, stopping when she saw the master and Aberdeen walking away. What would happen to her son next, she wondered. Unless she overheard a conversation in the main house, she would just have to wait and see.

A subdued atmosphere hung about the Moody residence for the rest of the day. Even Daniel Moody, who was usually lighthearted, seemed distressed enough to seek out his father. The two Moody men generally used the time prior to the evening meal to discuss their respective schedules, but tonight, Aberdeen was on Daniel's mind.

"Father," Daniel began cautiously, "what are your plans for Aberdeen's future, if I may be so bold as to ask?"

"What concern is it of yours?" his father answered gruffly.

"Well, I did grow up with him, Father, right here in this very yard, and I don't understand why the punishment must be so harsh."

"Well, how else would you suggest we train the young servants? They must understand exactly what's expected of them."

"But isn't there a less painful way to do it?"

"Daniel, my boy, you really don't understand, do you? These people come from a very different culture. We don't know what they're thinking, and so far, a lashing seems to be the one thing that keeps them in line. Besides, Daniel, I take care never to leave a servant so injured that he cannot be of service...'tis only meant to be a reminder. You best concern yourself with the rules of the gentry."

And with that, Mr. Moody rose and headed toward the house for dinner. Daniel followed, his mind full of unanswered questions.

That night, as Molly and Mary settled down on their pallets they had trouble falling off to sleep. Aberdeen's situation still worried them. Cate and Rose did what they usually did at a time like this. They told a story drawn from their African heritage that somehow always made sense out of the sadness and drudgery around them.

Molly and Mary were up early Saturday
morning. Today they wanted to make sure their
work would be done in time for the gathering.
When Cate asked which of the girls would go to
the milliner's for Mrs. Moody, Molly jumped at
the chance. She might find out about Aberdeen if
she happened to meet Rippon. Molly felt a real
kinship to Rose's son. They were alike in a way—
both always getting into more trouble than
Rippon or Mary.

Across town, Rippon had pushed hard all morning, and at noontime the tavern was so busy that Mr. Wetherburn asked him to help serve. Rippon barely had time to notice who the patrons were. Then, he heard the unmistakable voice of Master Moody.

"So you need a new roof?" Mr. Moody inquired of his guest.

"Indeed," the man answered, "and an addition to my stable."

"Without looking over your property, I should guess that we could begin sometime next month. I'll need to bring a foreman back from my farm," Mr. Moody continued. "I've got a good fellow, Samuel's his name. He could have the job done in no time."

Rippon almost dropped a plate of oysters in Mr. Moody's lap. He could hardly believe what he had just heard. Master Moody owned only one Samuel, and that slave happened to be Rippon's father. Poppa's coming to town to live for a while!

After the noon meal was over, Rippon dashed out the back door of the tavern, eager to find a way to get the news to his mother. He had a list of errands to do. "Maybe I'll see one of my sisters," Rippon thought.

His thoughts drifted to his father hard at work on the plantation. Poppa's life will sure change for the better, he thought. Rippon would have a real father again, even if it was only a temporary arrangement. Samuel had never stayed with the family more than a night at a time.

Rippon felt a rush of warmth as he hurried down the street. He headed for the grocer's. The clock struck two as he was leaving the store, and luck was with him. Molly was walking into the milliner's next door.

"Psst, Molly, over here," Rippon said. Molly

stopped and stayed close to the fence. Slaves weren't supposed to stand idle or loiter in town, conversing like the gentry.

"What is it, Rippon? You got news about Aberdeen?" Molly asked.

"No, not yet. But you gotta tell Momma that I heard Master Moody say he is bringing Poppa back to do a big job in town. That means Poppa is gon' be here for a long time, not just overnight. Tell Momma right away, y'hear?"

Molly smiled and nodded. Then brother and sister quickly went their separate ways.

At the apothecary Rippon picked up some remedies for a patron who had taken sick in the middle of the night. Then he dropped off his packages at Wetherburn's and headed toward the governor's Palace. He hadn't managed to pick up any information about his friend Aberdeen. The only way he'd find out anything was to see for himself. He rushed across the green and stopped outside the livery entrance to the Palace. Within minutes, a coach came speeding up, and Rippon saw Aberdeen run to steady the horses. Rippon waited until the coast was clear and then slipped into the yard.

"Aberdeen," he whispered, "Is you all right?"

"I'm a little sore," Aberdeen answered, working steadily as he talked so as not to get into more trouble. "But Master Moody didn't hurt me bad. He say that he was gon' give me ten lashes…"

"Ten!" Rippon gasped.

"But that strap of his didn't hit me more than five. The rest of the time it just slapped away at the tree."

"You sho' is lucky that he didn't send you off to the fields."

"Everyone can't be as good as you, Rippon. I learned that a long time ago. I is also learnin' when to work and when to slow down. You ought to pace yo'self too, or you'll start makin' mistakes and get punished like me."

Rippon didn't want to argue. In fact, he had run out of time and needed to get back to Wetherburn's before his absence was noticed. "Well, I suppose we won't be seein' you at the gatherin'," he said, starting to leave. Aberdeen shook his head. "Even if I wasn't in trouble, I'd have to stay cause of the ball."

Everywhere, it seemed, folks were getting ready for Saturday evening festivities.

Molly rushed back from town with Mrs. Moody's last minute requests. As she bounded through the gate, she met Hannah in the yard.

"Hannah, you'll never guess who I just saw," Molly teased.

"You didn't," Hannah exclaimed, a flush coming to her cheeks. "You ran into Nicholas Hornsby! Where?"

"Getting fitted for a mighty fancy satin coat that I suppose he plans to wear to the ball tonight."

"Then he's going!"

"Suppose so," Molly answered. "He sho' is a fine looking man, strong and tall and did he ever smell good …like lilac water. I hope to see my young man tonight at the gatherin'." Molly quickly covered her mouth. "Oops," she said. "You won't let on there's a gatherin', will you, Hannah?"

"Of course not, Molly," Hannah assured her.

"I just wish Aberdeen could come. Do you know if he's still in town? We none of us knows what's become of him."

Hannah paused, looked around and measured her words carefully. "Well, Father sent him back to work, I know that much. But it doesn't look good. Father says he needs dependable servants. Maybe Aberdeen finally learned his lesson. Don't worry yourself too much."

"Molly, is you out there, girl?" Cate screamed at her daughter.

"Comin', Momma," Molly answered, running toward the kitchen.

"You is draggin' yo' tail again, girl, and we have the table to set and supper to serve up."

"Yes, Momma," Molly murmured, stifling her anger. She loved talking to Hannah and hearing about her genteel life. "Someday," Molly resolved, "when Hannah marries, the master will send me to work for her. Then maybe I'll be able to make my own rules and not have to take orders from Momma." She followed her mother and Mary into the main house.

"What kept you in town so long?" Cate asked.

"I saw Rippon, Momma," Molly answered.

"Is that so?" Cate replied. "What is he up to?"

"He told me Poppa's comin' home," Molly said coyly.

"I know he's comin', child. Why you suppose I've been carrying on these past two days—wantin' to be sure we was ready for him."

"Well, we ain't gon' have to be so crazy from now on," Molly answered.

"What you talkin' about?" Cate asked, puzzled now at Molly's cunning.

"Rippon tell me Poppa's comin' home for the winter. Master Moody need him here for some buildin'."

"Well, that is some news, girl," Cate said, stifling her smile and trying hard not to be excited. "I ain't believin' nothin' till I talk to yo' poppa," she answered, her head filling up with questions, her heart beating heavily.

In the next room, Hannah was trying to concentrate as her mother began a lesson on serving tea. Hannah's mind was on one thing, Nicholas Hornsby. As her mother explained each step of the tea service, Hannah went through the motions but she wasn't really listening.

"Now, then, you try it, dear," her mother suggested.

"Huh? What?" Hannah stammered.

"Hannah, dear, are you all right? You do look a bit drawn. Are you sure you're up to going to the ball this evening?"

"Oh, yes, Mother!" Hannah exclaimed, "Now, where were we?"

They continued for the next half hour until Mrs. Moody left to dress for the ball. Hannah leaned back in her chair and grinned. "Finally," she said aloud and rang the bell to have Mary clear the dishes.

The sun was starting to drop behind the slave quarters as Molly raced to and fro with tray after tray of empty dishes from the Moody supper.

"Molly, is that you out there?" Rose called from Mrs. Moody's bedroom.

"I need my sewing basket something fierce. Fetch it for me, please."

"Now I get my orders from Rose," Molly thought as she approached the master bedroom and peered inside. There stood Mrs. Moody in a bright pink dress, waiting, Molly supposed, to be sewn into it. It was Mrs. Moody's first Palace ball and she had had a special gown made. Molly could see it all now…Mrs. Moody alighting from the carriage, the butler taking her cape, the Moody women dancing into the night.

"Molly!" Rose yelled, "Stop that daydreaming and do as you is told."

Molly raced to the quarters just in time to see —Poppa!

"Samuel," her mother cried out, "you is finally here!"

"You see me, don't you?" he replied as he gathered his wife into his arms.

"How did you get here so soon?" Cate asked. "You always come at dark."

"Hopped aboard a farm cart this time so I got plenty of energy for the gatherin'. You and I is gon' out dance everybody," he winked at his wife. "And I've a surprise for you."

"You do?" Cate asked, wondering if he had heard of Master Moody's new plans for him.

"I is home now for the winter. Gon' to be doing some buildin'."

"Oh, Samuel," Cate answered, acting as if this was the first time she had heard it. They walked off toward the backyard together. Molly felt warm and happy as she rushed to find Rose's sewing basket. So many good things had happened today, and soon Rippon would be home to join the family for dinner.

A few hours later, slaves from other households in town began to arrive for the gathering. Tonight they could leave behind the drudgery of their everyday lives. It was one of their few evenings of freedom—a chance to rekindle their spirits.

Soon the singing and dancing and stories and sharing would begin and continue well into the night. For a brief time, life would be good in the slave quarters of one Williamsburg household.

Our Thanks

We are most grateful to Colonial Williamsburg and, in particular, to Dennis O'Toole, vice president of Historic Area Programs. He encouraged our project because it depicted the life-style on the main streets and in the backyards in this eighteenth-century town. Our story, which is fiction, takes place about 1770. Dennis offered support staff in the way of interpreters and researchers and arranged for the use of numerous facilities.

Our conversations with Rex Ellis, assistant director for Black Programs, Kevin Kelly, a Williamsburg historian, and Dylan Pritchett, supervisor of Afro-American Programs, contributed immensely to the book's historical accuracy in its characters and their life situations.

Connie Graft from Interpretive Planning coordinated this massive effort. While on location with us, she removed obstacles from scenes about to be photographed, arranged for interpreters, and produced props whenever we needed them.

Barnie Barnes of the Company of Colonial Performers was indispensable from the preliminary stages through to the finished product. He helped us fashion a storyline around characters already created by the Colonial Performers.

Others who helped were Bill White, Mary Wiseman, Dorothy Poucher, Richard Nicoll, and Willie Fitz.

And finally, the cast of characters—the dedicated interpreters who bring to life colonial situations. Many thanks to our Williamsburg household:

Aberdeen—Alfred McQueen, *Cate*—Marilyn Taylor, *Daniel*—Daniel Fuchs, *Hannah*—Holly Canada, *Mary*—Joy Griffin, *Molly*—Jamillah Griffin, *Mr. Moody*—Gerry Fisher, *Mrs. Moody*—Kristen Everly, *Rippon*—Gregory Johnson, *Rose*—Bridgette Jackson, *Samuel*—Dylan Pritchett

*Joan Anderson and
George Ancona*